AF442903

Empowered Every Day

31-Day Planner &
Gratitude Journal

BEING
YOU
IS YOUR
power

Daily Planner

Date: S M T W T F S

Positive mind

My Goals for Today Are:

- ☐
- ☐
- ☐

My Schedule for Today is:

06:00

07:00

08:00

09:00

10:00

11:00

12:00

13:00

14:00

15:00

16:00

17:00

18:00

This morning I feel:

Notes:

PRACTICE MAKES progress

Rethink Negativity

Negative Thought	Positive Thought

Every Day is a New Beginning

Daily Reflections

Date: S M T W T F S

MOOD	AWESOME	GOOD	NEUTRAL	BAD	TERRIBLE
DAY #1					

HOURS OF SLEEP

1	2	3	4	5	6	7	8	9	10	11	12

DREAMS

SELF-LOVE

- ____________________
- ____________________
- ____________________
- ____________________

I FEEL BETTER BECAUSE

____
____
____
____

MY VISION BOARD

Make Today Better

Today I'm Grateful for:

____
____

Daily Planner

Date: S M T W T F S

Positive mind

My Goals for Today Are:

☐ _______________________________

☐ _______________________________

☐ _______________________________

My Schedule for Today is:

06:00

07:00

08:00

09:00

10:00

11:00

12:00

13:00

14:00

15:00

16:00

17:00

18:00

This morning I feel:

Notes:

PRACTICE MAKES progress

Rethink Negativity

Negative Thought	Positive Thought

Every Day is a New Beginning

Daily Reflections

Date: S M T W T F S

MOOD	AWESOME	GOOD	NEUTRAL	BAD	TERRIBLE
DAY #1					

HOURS OF SLEEP

1	2	3	4	5	6	7	8	9	10	11	12

DREAMS

SELF-LOVE

- ○ _______________
- ○ _______________
- ○ _______________
- ○ _______________

I FEEL BETTER BECAUSE

____
____
____
____

MY VISION BOARD

make Today Better

Today I'm Grateful for:

____
____
____

Daily Planner

Date: S M T W T F S

Positive mind

My Goals for Today Are:

- [ ] ___________________________
- [ ] ___________________________
- [ ] ___________________________

My Schedule for Today is:

06:00

07:00

08:00

09:00

10:00

11:00

12:00

13:00

14:00

15:00

16:00

17:00

18:00

This morning I feel:

Notes:

PRACTICE MAKES progress

Rethink Negativity

Negative Thought	Positive Thought

Every Day is a New Beginning

Daily Reflections

Date: S M T W T F S

MOOD	AWESOME	GOOD	NEUTRAL	BAD	TERRIBLE
DAY #1					

HOURS OF SLEEP

1	2	3	4	5	6	7	8	9	10	11	12

DREAMS

SELF-LOVE

- ○ ______________________
- ○ ______________________
- ○ ______________________
- ○ ______________________

I FEEL BETTER BECAUSE

____

____

____

____

MY VISION BOARD

Today I'm Grateful for:

____

____

____

Daily Planner

Date: S M T W T F S

Positive
mind

My Goals for Today Are:

- ☐
- ☐
- ☐

My Schedule for Today is:

06:00

07:00

08:00

09:00

10:00

11:00

12:00

13:00

14:00

15:00

16:00

17:00

18:00

This morning I feel:

Notes:

PRACTICE
MAKES
progress

Rethink Negativity

Negative Thought	Positive Thought

Every Day is a New Beginning

Daily Reflections

Date: S M T W T F S

MOOD	AWESOME	GOOD	NEUTRAL	BAD	TERRIBLE
DAY #1					

HOURS OF SLEEP

| 1 | 2 | 3 | 4 | 5 | 6 | 7 | 8 | 9 | 10 | 11 | 12 |

DREAMS

SELF-LOVE

○ ______________________________

○ ______________________________

○ ______________________________

○ ______________________________

I FEEL BETTER BECAUSE

MY VISION BOARD

Make Today Better

Today I'm Grateful for:

____

____

____

Daily Planner

Date: S M T W T F S

Positive mind

My Goals for Today Are:

- ☐ __________________________________
- ☐ __________________________________
- ☐ __________________________________

My Schedule for Today is:

06:00

07:00

08:00

09:00

10:00

11:00

12:00

13:00

14:00

15:00

16:00

17:00

18:00

This morning I feel:

Notes:

PRACTICE MAKES progress

Rethink Negativity

Negative Thought	Positive Thought

Every Day is a New Beginning

Daily Reflections

Date: S M T W T F S

MOOD	AWESOME	GOOD	NEUTRAL	BAD	TERRIBLE
DAY #1					

HOURS OF SLEEP

1	2	3	4	5	6	7	8	9	10	11	12

DREAMS

SELF-LOVE

I FEEL BETTER BECAUSE

MY VISION BOARD

Today I'm Grateful for:

Daily Planner

Date: S M T W T F S

Positive mind

My Goals for Today Are:

- ☐ _______________________
- ☐ _______________________
- ☐ _______________________

My Schedule for Today is:

06:00 _______________________
07:00 _______________________
08:00 _______________________
09:00 _______________________
10:00 _______________________
11:00 _______________________
12:00 _______________________
13:00 _______________________
14:00 _______________________
15:00 _______________________
16:00 _______________________
17:00 _______________________
18:00 _______________________

This morning I feel:

____
____
____
____

Notes:

____
____
____
____

PRACTICE MAKES progress

Rethink Negativity

Negative Thought	Positive Thought

Every Day is a New Beginning

Daily Reflections

Date: S M T W T F S

MOOD	AWESOME	GOOD	NEUTRAL	BAD	TERRIBLE
DAY #1					

HOURS OF SLEEP

1	2	3	4	5	6	7	8	9	10	11	12

DREAMS

SELF-LOVE

○ ___________________________________

○ ___________________________________

○ ___________________________________

○ ___________________________________

I FEEL BETTER BECAUSE

____

____

____

MY VISION BOARD

Make Today Better

Today I'm Grateful for:

____

____

____

Daily Planner

Date: S M T W T F S

Positive *mind*

My Goals for Today Are:

- [ ]
- [ ]
- [ ]

My Schedule for Today is:

06:00
07:00
08:00
09:00
10:00
11:00
12:00
13:00
14:00
15:00
16:00
17:00
18:00

This morning I feel:

Notes:

PRACTICE MAKES *progress*

Rethink Negativity

Negative Thought	Positive Thought

Every Day is a New Beginning

Daily Reflections

Date: S M T W T F S

MOOD	AWESOME	GOOD	NEUTRAL	BAD	TERRIBLE
DAY #1					

HOURS OF SLEEP

1	2	3	4	5	6	7	8	9	10	11	12

DREAMS

SELF-LOVE

I FEEL BETTER BECAUSE

MY VISION BOARD

Today I'm Grateful for:

Daily Planner

Positive mind

Date: S M T W T F S

My Goals for Today Are:

- [ ]
- [ ]
- [ ]

My Schedule for Today is:

06:00
07:00
08:00
09:00
10:00
11:00
12:00
13:00
14:00
15:00
16:00
17:00
18:00

This morning I feel:

Notes:

PRACTICE MAKES progress

Rethink Negativity

Negative Thought	Positive Thought

Every Day is a New Beginning

Daily Reflections

Date: S M T W T F S

MOOD	AWESOME	GOOD	NEUTRAL	BAD	TERRIBLE
DAY #1					

HOURS OF SLEEP

| 1 | 2 | 3 | 4 | 5 | 6 | 7 | 8 | 9 | 10 | 11 | 12 |

DREAMS

SELF-LOVE

I FEEL BETTER BECAUSE

MY VISION BOARD

Today I'm Grateful for:

Daily Planner

Date: S M T W T F S

Positive mind

My Goals for Today Are:

- [ ]
- [ ]
- [ ]

My Schedule for Today is:

06:00
07:00
08:00
09:00
10:00
11:00
12:00
13:00
14:00
15:00
16:00
17:00
18:00

This morning I feel:

Notes:

PRACTICE MAKES progress

Rethink Negativity

Negative Thought	Positive Thought

Every Day is a New Beginning

Daily Reflections

Date: S M T W T F S

MOOD	AWESOME	GOOD	NEUTRAL	BAD	TERRIBLE
DAY #1					

HOURS OF SLEEP

1	2	3	4	5	6	7	8	9	10	11	12

DREAMS

SELF-LOVE

I FEEL BETTER BECAUSE

MY VISION BOARD

Today I'm Grateful for:

Daily Planner

Date: S M T W T F S

Positive mind

My Goals for Today Are:

- ☐
- ☐
- ☐

My Schedule for Today is:

06:00
07:00
08:00
09:00
10:00
11:00
12:00
13:00
14:00
15:00
16:00
17:00
18:00

This morning I feel:

Notes:

PRACTICE MAKES progress

Rethink Negativity

Negative Thought	Positive Thought

Every Day is a New Beginning

Daily Reflections

Date: S M T W T F S

MOOD	AWESOME	GOOD	NEUTRAL	BAD	TERRIBLE
DAY #1					

HOURS OF SLEEP

| 1 | 2 | 3 | 4 | 5 | 6 | 7 | 8 | 9 | 10 | 11 | 12 |

DREAMS

SELF-LOVE

- ○ ________________________
- ○ ________________________
- ○ ________________________
- ○ ________________________

I FEEL BETTER BECAUSE

____
____
____
____

MY VISION BOARD

Make Today Better

Today I'm Grateful for:

____
____
____

Daily Planner

Date: S M T W T F S

Positive mind

My Goals for Today Are:

☐ _______________________________

☐ _______________________________

☐ _______________________________

My Schedule for Today is:

06:00 _______________________

07:00 _______________________

08:00 _______________________

09:00 _______________________

10:00 _______________________

11:00 _______________________

12:00 _______________________

13:00 _______________________

14:00 _______________________

15:00 _______________________

16:00 _______________________

17:00 _______________________

18:00 _______________________

This morning I feel:

____

____

____

____

Notes:

____

____

____

____

PRACTICE MAKES progress

Rethink Negativity

Negative Thought	Positive Thought

Every Day is a New Beginning

Daily Reflections

Date: S M T W T F S

MOOD	AWESOME	GOOD	NEUTRAL	BAD	TERRIBLE
DAY #1					

HOURS OF SLEEP

1	2	3	4	5	6	7	8	9	10	11	12

DREAMS

SELF-LOVE

○ ____________________
○ ____________________
○ ____________________
○ ____________________

I FEEL BETTER BECAUSE

____
____
____
____

MY VISION BOARD

Today I'm Grateful for:

____

____

____

Daily Planner

Positive mind

Date: S M T W T F S

My Goals for Today Are:

☐ ___________________________

☐ ___________________________

☐ ___________________________

My Schedule for Today is:

06:00

07:00

08:00

09:00

10:00

11:00

12:00

13:00

14:00

15:00

16:00

17:00

18:00

This morning I feel:

Notes:

PRACTICE MAKES progress

Rethink Negativity

Negative Thought	Positive Thought

Every Day is a New Beginning

Daily Reflections

Date: S M T W T F S

MOOD	AWESOME	GOOD	NEUTRAL	BAD	TERRIBLE
DAY #1					

HOURS OF SLEEP

1	2	3	4	5	6	7	8	9	10	11	12

DREAMS

SELF-LOVE

I FEEL BETTER BECAUSE

MY VISION BOARD

Today I'm Grateful for:

Daily Planner

Date: S M T W T F S

Positive mind

My Goals for Today Are:

☐ _______________________________

☐ _______________________________

☐ _______________________________

My Schedule for Today is:

06:00 _______________________________

07:00 _______________________________

08:00 _______________________________

09:00 _______________________________

10:00 _______________________________

11:00 _______________________________

12:00 _______________________________

13:00 _______________________________

14:00 _______________________________

15:00 _______________________________

16:00 _______________________________

17:00 _______________________________

18:00 _______________________________

This morning I feel:

____

____

____

Notes:

____

____

____

____

____

Practice Makes progress

Rethink Negativity

Negative Thought	Positive Thought

Every Day is a New Beginning

Daily Reflections

Date: S M T W T F S

MOOD	AWESOME	GOOD	NEUTRAL	BAD	TERRIBLE
DAY #1					

HOURS OF SLEEP

| 1 | 2 | 3 | 4 | 5 | 6 | 7 | 8 | 9 | 10 | 11 | 12 |

DREAMS

SELF-LOVE

-
-
-
-

I FEEL BETTER BECAUSE

MY VISION BOARD

Today I'm Grateful for:

Daily Planner

Date: S M T W T F S

Positive mind

My Goals for Today Are:

☐

☐

☐

My Schedule for Today is:

06:00

07:00

08:00

09:00

10:00

11:00

12:00

13:00

14:00

15:00

16:00

17:00

18:00

This morning I feel:

Notes:

PRACTICE MAKES progress

Rethink Negativity

Negative Thought	Positive Thought

Every Day is a New Beginning

Daily Reflections

Date: S M T W T F S

MOOD	AWESOME	GOOD	NEUTRAL	BAD	TERRIBLE
DAY #1					

HOURS OF SLEEP

1	2	3	4	5	6	7	8	9	10	11	12

DREAMS

SELF-LOVE

○ _______________________
○ _______________________
○ _______________________
○ _______________________

I FEEL BETTER BECAUSE

MY VISION BOARD

Make Today Better

Today I'm Grateful for:

Daily Planner

Date: S M T W T F S

Positive mind

My Goals for Today Are:

- [ ]
- [ ]
- [ ]

My Schedule for Today is:

06:00

07:00

08:00

09:00

10:00

11:00

12:00

13:00

14:00

15:00

16:00

17:00

18:00

This morning I feel:

Notes:

PRACTICE MAKES progress

Rethink Negativity

Negative Thought	Positive Thought

Every Day is a New Beginning

Daily Reflections

Date: S M T W T F S

MOOD	AWESOME	GOOD	NEUTRAL	BAD	TERRIBLE
DAY #1					

HOURS OF SLEEP

| 1 | 2 | 3 | 4 | 5 | 6 | 7 | 8 | 9 | 10 | 11 | 12 |

DREAMS

SELF-LOVE

- ___________________________
- ___________________________
- ___________________________
- ___________________________

I FEEL BETTER BECAUSE

____
____
____
____

MY VISION BOARD

Today I'm Grateful for:

____
____

Daily Planner

Date: S M T W T F S

Positive mind

My Goals for Today Are:

- [ ]
- [ ]
- [ ]

My Schedule for Today is:

06:00

07:00

08:00

09:00

10:00

11:00

12:00

13:00

14:00

15:00

16:00

17:00

18:00

This morning I feel:

Notes:

Practice MAKES progress

Rethink Negativity

Negative Thought	Positive Thought

Every Day is a New Beginning

Daily Reflections

Date: S M T W T F S

MOOD	AWESOME	GOOD	NEUTRAL	BAD	TERRIBLE
DAY #1					

HOURS OF SLEEP

1	2	3	4	5	6	7	8	9	10	11	12

DREAMS

SELF-LOVE

- ◯ ________________________
- ◯ ________________________
- ◯ ________________________
- ◯ ________________________

I FEEL BETTER BECAUSE

____
____
____
____

MY VISION BOARD

Make Today Better

Today I'm Grateful for:

____
____
____

Daily Planner

Date: S M T W T F S

Positive mind

My Goals for Today Are:

- [ ] ________________________________
- [ ] ________________________________
- [ ] ________________________________

My Schedule for Today is:

06:00 ________________________________
07:00 ________________________________
08:00 ________________________________
09:00 ________________________________
10:00 ________________________________
11:00 ________________________________
12:00 ________________________________
13:00 ________________________________
14:00 ________________________________
15:00 ________________________________
16:00 ________________________________
17:00 ________________________________
18:00 ________________________________

This morning I feel:

____

____

____

____

Notes:

____

____

____

____

PRACTICE MAKES progress

Rethink Negativity

Negative Thought	Positive Thought

Every Day is a New Beginning

Daily Reflections

Date: S M T W T F S

MOOD	AWESOME	GOOD	NEUTRAL	BAD	TERRIBLE
DAY #1					

HOURS OF SLEEP

1	2	3	4	5	6	7	8	9	10	11	12

DREAMS

SELF-LOVE

- ○ _______________________________
- ○ _______________________________
- ○ _______________________________
- ○ _______________________________

I FEEL BETTER BECAUSE

MY VISION BOARD

Today I'm Grateful for:

Daily Planner

Date: S M T W T F S

Positive mind

My Goals for Today Are:

- [ ] ______________________________
- [ ] ______________________________
- [ ] ______________________________

My Schedule for Today is:

06:00 ______________________________
07:00 ______________________________
08:00 ______________________________
09:00 ______________________________
10:00 ______________________________
11:00 ______________________________
12:00 ______________________________
13:00 ______________________________
14:00 ______________________________
15:00 ______________________________
16:00 ______________________________
17:00 ______________________________
18:00 ______________________________

This morning I feel:

____

____

____

____

Notes:

____

____

____

____

Practice MAKES progress

Rethink Negativity

Negative Thought	Positive Thought

Every Day is a New Beginning

Daily Reflections

Date: S M T W T F S

MOOD	AWESOME	GOOD	NEUTRAL	BAD	TERRIBLE
DAY #1					

HOURS OF SLEEP

| 1 | 2 | 3 | 4 | 5 | 6 | 7 | 8 | 9 | 10 | 11 | 12 |

DREAMS

SELF-LOVE

I FEEL BETTER BECAUSE

MY VISION BOARD

Today I'm Grateful for:

Daily Planner

Date: S M T W T F S

Positive mind

My Goals for Today Are:

- [ ]
- [ ]
- [ ]

My Schedule for Today is:

06:00	
07:00	
08:00	
09:00	
10:00	
11:00	
12:00	
13:00	
14:00	
15:00	
16:00	
17:00	
18:00	

This morning I feel:

Notes:

PRACTICE MAKES progress

Rethink Negativity

Negative Thought	Positive Thought

Every Day is a New Beginning

Daily Reflections

Date: S M T W T F S

MOOD	AWESOME	GOOD	NEUTRAL	BAD	TERRIBLE
DAY #1					

HOURS OF SLEEP

1	2	3	4	5	6	7	8	9	10	11	12

DREAMS

SELF-LOVE

- ◯ ________________________
- ◯ ________________________
- ◯ ________________________
- ◯ ________________________

I FEEL BETTER BECAUSE

____

____

____

____

MY VISION BOARD

Make Today Better

Today I'm Grateful for:

____

____

____

Daily Planner

Date: S M T W T F S

Positive mind

My Goals for Today Are:

☐ ____

☐ ____

☐ ____

My Schedule for Today is:

06:00 ___________________________________

07:00 ___________________________________

08:00 ___________________________________

09:00 ___________________________________

10:00 ___________________________________

11:00 ___________________________________

12:00 ___________________________________

13:00 ___________________________________

14:00 ___________________________________

15:00 ___________________________________

16:00 ___________________________________

17:00 ___________________________________

18:00 ___________________________________

This morning I feel:

____

____

____

____

Notes:

____

____

____

____

PRACTICE MAKES progress

Rethink Negativity

Negative Thought	Positive Thought

Every Day is a New Beginning

Daily Reflections

Date: S M T W T F S

MOOD	AWESOME	GOOD	NEUTRAL	BAD	TERRIBLE
DAY #1					

HOURS OF SLEEP

1	2	3	4	5	6	7	8	9	10	11	12

DREAMS

SELF-LOVE

- ____________________
- ____________________
- ____________________
- ____________________

I FEEL BETTER BECAUSE

____
____
____
____

MY VISION BOARD

Today I'm Grateful for:

____
____
____

Daily Planner

Date: S M T W T F S

Positive mind

My Goals for Today Are:

- [ ]
- [ ]
- [ ]

My Schedule for Today is:

06:00
07:00
08:00
09:00
10:00
11:00
12:00
13:00
14:00
15:00
16:00
17:00
18:00

This morning I feel:

Notes:

PRACTICE MAKES progress

Rethink Negativity

Negative Thought	Positive Thought

Every Day is a New Beginning

Daily Reflections

Date: S M T W T F S

MOOD	AWESOME	GOOD	NEUTRAL	BAD	TERRIBLE
DAY #1					

HOURS OF SLEEP

| 1 | 2 | 3 | 4 | 5 | 6 | 7 | 8 | 9 | 10 | 11 | 12 |

DREAMS

SELF-LOVE

-
-
-
-

I FEEL BETTER BECAUSE

MY VISION BOARD

Today I'm Grateful for:

Daily Planner

Date: S M T W T F S

Positive mind

My Goals for Today Are:

- ☐
- ☐
- ☐

My Schedule for Today is:

06:00
07:00
08:00
09:00
10:00
11:00
12:00
13:00
14:00
15:00
16:00
17:00
18:00

This morning I feel:

Notes:

PRACTICE MAKES progress

Rethink Negativity

Negative Thought	Positive Thought

Every Day is a New Beginning

Daily Reflections

Date: S   M   T   W   T   F   S

MOOD	AWESOME	GOOD	NEUTRAL	BAD	TERRIBLE
DAY #1					

HOURS OF SLEEP

1	2	3	4	5	6	7	8	9	10	11	12

DREAMS

SELF-LOVE

- ___________________________
- ___________________________
- ___________________________
- ___________________________

I FEEL BETTER BECAUSE

____
____
____
____

MY VISION BOARD

Today I'm Grateful for:

____

____

____

Daily Planner

Date: S M T W T F S

Positive mind

My Goals for Today Are:

- [ ]
- [ ]
- [ ]

My Schedule for Today is:

06:00

07:00

08:00

09:00

10:00

11:00

12:00

13:00

14:00

15:00

16:00

17:00

18:00

This morning I feel:

Notes:

PRACTICE MAKES progress

Rethink Negativity

Negative Thought	Positive Thought

Every Day is a New Beginning

Daily Reflections

Date: S M T W T F S

MOOD	AWESOME	GOOD	NEUTRAL	BAD	TERRIBLE
DAY #1					

HOURS OF SLEEP

1	2	3	4	5	6	7	8	9	10	11	12

DREAMS

SELF-LOVE

- ○ __________________________
- ○ __________________________
- ○ __________________________
- ○ __________________________

I FEEL BETTER BECAUSE

____
____
____
____

MY VISION BOARD

Make Today Better

Today I'm Grateful for:

____
____

Daily Planner

Date: S M T W T F S

Positive mind

My Goals for Today Are:

☐ ______________________________

☐ ______________________________

☐ ______________________________

My Schedule for Today is:

06:00 ______________________________

07:00 ______________________________

08:00 ______________________________

09:00 ______________________________

10:00 ______________________________

11:00 ______________________________

12:00 ______________________________

13:00 ______________________________

14:00 ______________________________

15:00 ______________________________

16:00 ______________________________

17:00 ______________________________

18:00 ______________________________

This morning I feel:

Notes:

PRACTICE MAKES progress

Rethink Negativity

Negative Thought	Positive Thought

Every Day is a New Beginning

Daily Reflections

Date: S M T W T F S

MOOD	AWESOME	GOOD	NEUTRAL	BAD	TERRIBLE
DAY #1					

HOURS OF SLEEP

1	2	3	4	5	6	7	8	9	10	11	12

DREAMS

SELF-LOVE

- ____________________
- ____________________
- ____________________
- ____________________

I FEEL BETTER BECAUSE

____
____
____
____

MY VISION BOARD

Today I'm Grateful for:

____
____
____

Daily Planner

Date: S M T W T F S

Positive mind

My Goals for Today Are:

- [ ]
- [ ]
- [ ]

My Schedule for Today is:

06:00

07:00

08:00

09:00

10:00

11:00

12:00

13:00

14:00

15:00

16:00

17:00

18:00

This morning I feel:

Notes:

PRACTICE MAKES progress

Rethink Negativity

Negative Thought	Positive Thought

Every Day is a New Beginning

Daily Reflections

Date: S M T W T F S

MOOD	AWESOME	GOOD	NEUTRAL	BAD	TERRIBLE
DAY #1					

HOURS OF SLEEP

1	2	3	4	5	6	7	8	9	10	11	12

DREAMS

SELF-LOVE

○ ___________________________
○ ___________________________
○ ___________________________
○ ___________________________

I FEEL BETTER BECAUSE

____
____
____
____

MY VISION BOARD

Today I'm Grateful for:

____

____

____

Daily Planner

Date: S M T W T F S

My Goals for Today Are:

- ☐
- ☐
- ☐

My Schedule for Today is:

06:00
07:00
08:00
09:00
10:00
11:00
12:00
13:00
14:00
15:00
16:00
17:00
18:00

This morning I feel:

Notes:

Rethink Negativity

Negative Thought	Positive Thought

Every Day is a New Beginning

Daily Reflections

Date: S M T W T F S

MOOD	AWESOME	GOOD	NEUTRAL	BAD	TERRIBLE
DAY #1					

HOURS OF SLEEP

1	2	3	4	5	6	7	8	9	10	11	12

DREAMS

SELF-LOVE

○ _______________

○ _______________

○ _______________

○ _______________

I FEEL BETTER BECAUSE

MY VISION BOARD

make Today Better

Today I'm Grateful for:

____

____

Daily Planner

Date: S M T W T F S

Positive mind

My Goals for Today Are:

- ☐ _______________________
- ☐ _______________________
- ☐ _______________________

My Schedule for Today is:

06:00 _______________________
07:00 _______________________
08:00 _______________________
09:00 _______________________
10:00 _______________________
11:00 _______________________
12:00 _______________________
13:00 _______________________
14:00 _______________________
15:00 _______________________
16:00 _______________________
17:00 _______________________
18:00 _______________________

This morning I feel:

____

Notes:

____

PRACTICE MAKES progress

Rethink Negativity

Negative Thought	Positive Thought

Every Day is a New Beginning

Daily Reflections

Date: S M T W T F S

MOOD	AWESOME	GOOD	NEUTRAL	BAD	TERRIBLE
DAY #1					

HOURS OF SLEEP

| 1 | 2 | 3 | 4 | 5 | 6 | 7 | 8 | 9 | 10 | 11 | 12 |

DREAMS

SELF-LOVE

- ◯ __________
- ◯ __________
- ◯ __________
- ◯ __________

I FEEL BETTER BECAUSE

____
____
____
____

MY VISION BOARD

Today I'm Grateful for:

____
____
____

Daily Planner

Date: S M T W T F S

Positive mind

My Goals for Today Are:

☐ ___________________________

☐ ___________________________

☐ ___________________________

My Schedule for Today is:

06:00 ___________________________

07:00 ___________________________

08:00 ___________________________

09:00 ___________________________

10:00 ___________________________

11:00 ___________________________

12:00 ___________________________

13:00 ___________________________

14:00 ___________________________

15:00 ___________________________

16:00 ___________________________

17:00 ___________________________

18:00 ___________________________

This morning I feel:

____

____

____

____

Notes:

____

____

____

____

____

PRACTICE MAKES progress

Rethink Negativity

Negative Thought	Positive Thought

Every Day is a New Beginning

Daily Reflections

Date: S M T W T F S

MOOD	AWESOME	GOOD	NEUTRAL	BAD	TERRIBLE
DAY #1					

HOURS OF SLEEP

1	2	3	4	5	6	7	8	9	10	11	12

DREAMS

SELF-LOVE

- ___________________________
- ___________________________
- ___________________________
- ___________________________

I FEEL BETTER BECAUSE

____
____
____
____

MY VISION BOARD

Today I'm Grateful for:

____
____
____

Daily Planner

Date: S M T W T F S

Positive mind

My Goals for Today Are:

- [ ]
- [ ]
- [ ]

My Schedule for Today is:

06:00
07:00
08:00
09:00
10:00
11:00
12:00
13:00
14:00
15:00
16:00
17:00
18:00

This morning I feel:

Notes:

PRACTICE MAKES progress

Rethink Negativity

Negative Thought	Positive Thought

Every Day is a New Beginning

Daily Reflections

Date: S M T W T F S

MOOD	AWESOME	GOOD	NEUTRAL	BAD	TERRIBLE
DAY #1					

HOURS OF SLEEP

| 1 | 2 | 3 | 4 | 5 | 6 | 7 | 8 | 9 | 10 | 11 | 12 |

DREAMS

SELF-LOVE

- ___________________________
- ___________________________
- ___________________________
- ___________________________

I FEEL BETTER BECAUSE

____
____
____
____

MY VISION BOARD

Make Today Better

Today I'm Grateful for:

____
____
____

Daily Planner

Date: S M T W T F S

Positive mind

My Goals for Today Are:

- [ ]
- [ ]
- [ ]

My Schedule for Today is:

06:00
07:00
08:00
09:00
10:00
11:00
12:00
13:00
14:00
15:00
16:00
17:00
18:00

This morning I feel:

Notes:

PRACTICE MAKES progress

Rethink Negativity

Negative Thought	Positive Thought

Every Day is a New Beginning

Daily Reflections

Date: S M T W T F S

MOOD	AWESOME	GOOD	NEUTRAL	BAD	TERRIBLE
DAY #1					

HOURS OF SLEEP

1	2	3	4	5	6	7	8	9	10	11	12

DREAMS

SELF-LOVE

- ○ ____________________
- ○ ____________________
- ○ ____________________
- ○ ____________________

I FEEL BETTER BECAUSE

____
____
____
____

MY VISION BOARD

Today I'm Grateful for:

____
____
____

Daily Planner

Date: S M T W T F S

Positive mind

My Goals for Today Are:

- [ ]
- [ ]
- [ ]

My Schedule for Today is:

06:00

07:00

08:00

09:00

10:00

11:00

12:00

13:00

14:00

15:00

16:00

17:00

18:00

This morning I feel:

Notes:

Practice MAKES progress

Rethink Negativity

Negative Thought	Positive Thought

Every Day is a New Beginning

Daily Reflections

Date: S M T W T F S

MOOD	AWESOME	GOOD	NEUTRAL	BAD	TERRIBLE
DAY #1					

HOURS OF SLEEP

| 1 | 2 | 3 | 4 | 5 | 6 | 7 | 8 | 9 | 10 | 11 | 12 |

DREAMS

SELF-LOVE

○ _______________________________
○ _______________________________
○ _______________________________
○ _______________________________

I FEEL BETTER BECAUSE

____
____
____
____

MY VISION BOARD

Make Today Better

Today I'm Grateful for:

____
____
____

Daily Planner

Date: S M T W T F S

Positive mind

My Goals for Today Are:

- ☐ ____________________________
- ☐ ____________________________
- ☐ ____________________________

My Schedule for Today is:

06:00
07:00
08:00
09:00
10:00
11:00
12:00
13:00
14:00
15:00
16:00
17:00
18:00

This morning I feel:

Notes:

PRACTICE MAKES progress

Rethink Negativity

Negative Thought	Positive Thought

Every Day is a New Beginning

Daily Reflections

Date: S M T W T F S

MOOD	AWESOME	GOOD	NEUTRAL	BAD	TERRIBLE
DAY #1					

HOURS OF SLEEP

1	2	3	4	5	6	7	8	9	10	11	12

DREAMS

SELF-LOVE

I FEEL BETTER BECAUSE

MY VISION BOARD

Today I'm Grateful for:

Empowered Every Day

Enjoy the Journey